THE
BROWNING HI-POWER
PISTOLS

A comprehensive manual for the use, maintenance and repair of the various models of the Browning Hi-Power (P-35) 9mm Parabellum pistol, both military contract & commercial models.

By Donald B. McLean

DESERT PUBLICATIONS

ISBN: 0-87947-125-5

Library of Congress Catalog Card Number
65-27592

DESERT PUBLICATIONS
P.O. Box 22005
Phoenix, AZ 85028

Appreciation is expressed to the
following offices, who cooperated in the
compilation of technical and historical data:

Fabrique Nationale d' Armes de Guerre
Herstal-lez-Liege, Belgium

Her Majesty's War Office, Land Service,
Director of Infantry, London

Browning Arms Company, Morgan, Utah

TABLE OF CONTENTS:

ILLUSTRATIONS

INTRODUCTION

The Browning "Hi-Power" pistol is undoubtedly one of the finest automatic pistols ever developed. The last design to spring from the inventiveness of John M. Browning, it was patented in 1927, soon after his death.

The first model of this pistol to see official use was the French military model of 1935 in 9mm parabellum, as manufactured at Fabrique Nationale in Belgium. This is quite similar to most Hi-Powers found in general use, featuring the 13-shot magazine. It also had the fairly common tangent rear sight, and was fitted with a shoulder stock similar to the stock-holsters on early Mauser military pistols.

The Belgian government adopted a somewhat different model in the late 30's that had a shorter (10-shot) magazine, and a shortened slide. The Roumanians adopted a model similar to the French M-35 at about the same time. Thus when Belgium was overrun by the Nazis in the Second World War, FN was producing Hi-Powers in quantity. The Nazis held it in high regard as a military pistol, and some 200,000 were produced under German control. The Hi-Powers produced under Nazi occupation were subject to sabotage during manufacture, and the barrel nose, barrel nose seating, barrel locking lugs, and slide recesses should be closely examined on any Hi-Power showing Nazi proofs, to ascertain that all bearing and locking surfaces are correct.

A first cousin of the Hi-Power was developed in Poland in 1935 with the help of technicians from FN. Commonly called the "Radom" from its place of manufacture, it differs from the original Hi-Power in that it has an 8-shot magazine, grip safety, and a special hammer release mechanism.

Located on the left side of the slide, the release lever moves the floating firing pin forward and then drops the hammer harmlessly against the firing pin recess, merely as a safe way of lowering the hammer on a loaded chamber. Thousands of these Radoms were also produced under Nazi occupation when the Germans overran Poland, and many have been reported sabotaged to fire when the hammer release is tripped. If a Radom bears Nazi proofs, it should be checked for a firing pin that is too long, or hammer recess that is cut too deeply. This hammer release feature was left off many of the very late production Radoms, and on these the same barrel and slide areas as on the above Hi-Powers were often sabotaged. Hence, these points should also be checked on Nazi Radoms.

During the War many of the engineers from FN escaped to Canada, where they were instrumental in the John Inglis Company's tooling up to produce the Hi-Power pistol. Inglis manufactured quantities

of Hi-Powers for the Canadian and Chinese forces, and these were
of high quality production. Various quite similar models (varying
usually only in sights, stock fittings and other details) of the Hi-
Power pistol also have been adopted by Great Britain, many of the
NATO nations, and a number of smaller countries. The Hi-Power
is commercially manufactured at FN in Belgium, and is marketed in
the U.S. and Canada by the Browning Arms Company. The standard
commercial version as now being manufactured, and the military models used by the British are the most representative of the various Hi-
Powers, and as they also are the most likely to be encountered, it
is these that will be dealt with in depth in this manual. Variants as
made by FN for sale to various countries, and as manufactured under
Nazi control are to be expected, but they will usually differ only
in such matters as sights, fittings, lanyard rings and other obvious
and insignificant details.

Fig. "A"

Pistol, Browning, F.N. 9mm H.P., No 2, Mark I*
as currently issued by British forces

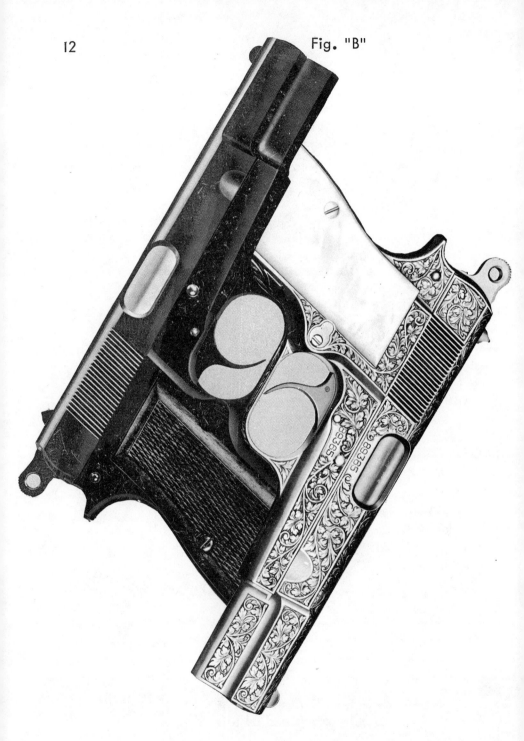

Current manufacture of the commercial Browning
Hi-Power pistol as done by Fabrique Nationale,
standard model, and engraved.

CHAPTER I, DESCRIPTION AND OPERATION

Section I, Description:

1. The Browning Hi-Power pistol is recoil operated, magazine fed, and self-loading. The breech is positively locked at the moment of firing. Fully automatic fire is impossible on standard models, the trigger must be pressed and released for each shot fired.

2. The rate of fire is limited by the ability of the user to load, aim and squeeze the trigger rapidly. Its short barrel allows it to be portable, handy and facilitates rapid engagement of suddenly exposed targets. It can be effectively used with either hand, and is especially useful at close quarters. When fitted with a shoulder stock, it has an accurate useable range of about 200 yards. When used as a pistol only, its useable range is about 50 yards.

3. Technical description:
    (a) Caliber-----------------------9mm Parabellum ("Luger")
    (b) Length of pistol----------------7, 3/4 inches
    (c) Length of barrel --------------4, 3/4 inches
    (d) Number of grooves -----------6
    (e) Pitch of rifling ---------------1 turn in 10 inches
    (f) Twist of rifling ---------------Right hand, concentric
    (g) Weights:
        (i) Pistol less magazine ---------1 pound, 15 ounces
        (ii) Magazine full---------------8 ounces
        (iii) Magazine empty -----------3 ounces
    (h) System of operation -----------Recoil
    (i) Sights:
        (i) Front ----------------------Barleycorn
        (ii)Rear-----------------------Square notched, or tangent adjustable to 500 meters
    (j) Sight radius-------------------6, 1/4 inches
    (k) Trigger pull ------------------5 to 8 pounds
    (l) Magazine capacity-----------13 rounds
    (m) Magazine type --------------Staggered row, box
    (n) Attachments----(some models)---Wooden holster-stock, lanyard ring

4. The pistol consists of five principal assemblies: the receiver (body), slide, barrel, mainspring guide, and magazine (Fig. 1).

5. The receiver, or body, is a one piece frame formed with a trigger guard and butt. It houses the firing mechanism and magazine and is machined to receive various components and pins. Inden-

tations in the shoulder at the top left of the butt receive the plunger of the safety catch to hold the catch at a set position. The upper sides are formed with guides at the center and rear to receive the slide, and inside the front end of the center guide is a U-shaped slide stop. A locking piece, which actuates the barrel, is fitted transversely below the center guide. The serial number is stamped on the right side of the receiver, and it should agree with those on the barrel and slide.

(a) The magazine catch (Fig. 2) is housed to the rear of the trigger guard, and engages a recess in the magazine to hold the magazine in position. It has a knurled thumb-piece and is retained in position by a spring-loaded plunger known as the retaining catch. The retaining catch plunger is housed in the magazine catch and a lug on its outer end engages a recess in the receiver to retain it in position.

(b) The slide locking lever (Fig. 2) is located on the left side of the receiver, its pin passing through the receiver. It is held in position by a recess in the pin engaging a retaining ball in the mainspring guide. At the rear end is a milled thumbpiece on the inner face of which is a lug that engages a recess in the slide to lock the slide.

(c) The butt (Fig. 2) forms the rear part of the receiver and houses the magazine. It also accomodates the hammer link assembly, sear, sear spring, ejector and safety catch. Side stocks (grips) are attached by screws, and in some models a lanyard loop is screwed in at the lower left. On other models the rear plane of the butt is slotted to accept the locking mechanism for the shoulder-stock attachment. Midway inside, at the rear, is a slotted step that serves as a seating for the hammer link spring and as a guide for the link. Inside at the bottom is a recess for the stud of the sear spring.

(d) The safety catch (Fig. 2) is located at the top left of the butt, and is retained by a lug formed on its pin. The pin passes through the receiver and the axis of the hammer. Housed in the milled thumb-piece is a spring-loaded plunger that holds the catch at a set position, and when it is applied the catch engages a recess in the slide, and a stud on its inner face locks the sear.

(e) The ejector (Fig. 2) is a plate held in position by the sear pin and on the pin of the safety catch. The top front projects forward in a groove in the slide so that the base of the cartridge case contacts it on recoil, and is thus ejected.

(f) The sear (Fig. 2) is retained by its axis pin at the top of the butt. One arm projects rearward to engage the hammer and the other projects downward and over the sear spring. A lug is formed on its left, which is engaged by the stud on the safety catch when it is applied.

(g) The sear spring (Fig. 2) is long and flat. The top end engages behind the sear, and the bottom end, formed with a stud,

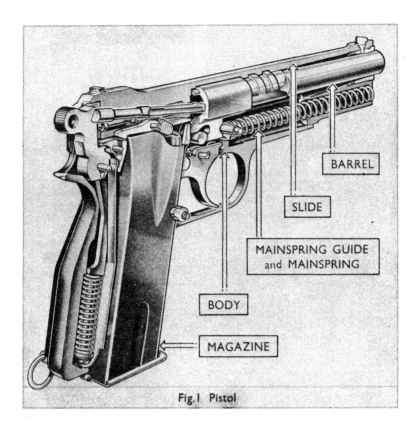

BARREL

SLIDE

MAINSPRING GUIDE
and MAINSPRING

BODY

MAGAZINE

Fig.1 Pistol

is seated in a recess in the bottom of the butt.

(h) The hammer link assembly (Fig. 2), consists of the hammer, hammer link, spring and retaining nut.

(i) The hammer is formed with two bents engaged by the sear when the hammer is cocked. It rotates on the pin of the safety catch; its axis hole is drilled through a hardened bush. The striking face is flat and the top rear is knurled to provide a better grip for the thumb.

(ii) The hammer link transmits the influence of the spring on the hammer. It pivots on a pin in the bush of the hammer and is positioned by means of the guide in the butt. Its lower part is screw-threaded to receive the retaining nut, and a step formed midway serves as a spring seating.

(iii) The spring is a coil spring, and fits over the lower part of the link. It is retained by a nut, which in turn is retained by a pin.

6. The slide group (Figs. 3 and 4), houses the barrel, mainspring guide, sear connecting arm, firing pin and extractor. A screwed

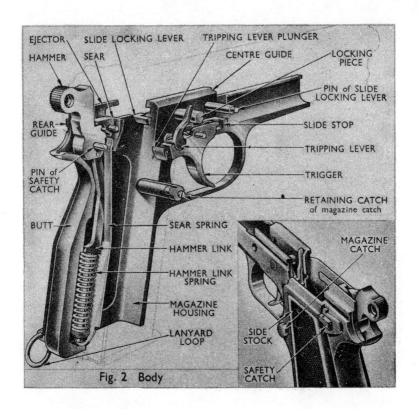

Fig. 2 Body

bush that serves as a bearing for the barrel is fitted at the front
and secured by a rivet, and below this is the mainspring seating.
Guideways are cut along the interior for the guides of the receiver
and an ejection opening is cut into the right side. Machined in the
left hand side are recesses that receive the slide locking lever and
safety catch when those units are applied. The back sight is machined or mounted in or on the top rear, and the fore sight is seated
in a dovetail at the top front.

(a) The firing pin housing is formed inside the slide at the rear.
Its front face is the cartridge seating, the lower part of which is
the feed piece, and a locking plate closes the rear end. The
plate, drilled to permit protrusion of the rear end of the firing pin,
retains the spring loaded firing pin within the housing and also secures
the extractor. Located along its length are the extractor and sear
connecting arm; the latter being secured by an arm pin located
through the right side of the slide. The arm pin is shaped to suit
the extractor which, in turn, locks the arm pin to the slide when in
position.

7. The barrel (Fig. 5), has a rifled bore with six grooves. Two

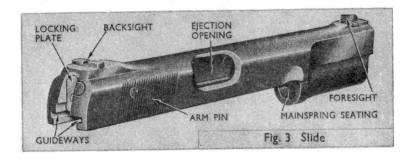

Fig. 3 Slide

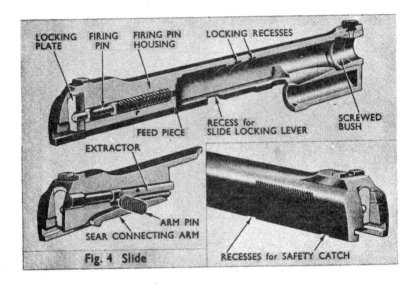

Fig. 4 Slide

external locking lugs are formed at the top rear, and a bullet guide and cam projection are formed below the breech end. In the rear of the cam projection is a slot that engages the locking piece to lock and unlock the barrel and in its front is a recess that receives the ring of the mainspring guide. A lug at the top rear of the chamber ensures correct alignment of the barrel in the locked position.

8. The mainspring guide (Fig. 6) accommodates the mainspring externally, and houses the slide locking lever spring, which is retained, under compression, by a screw plug. Towards the rear is a collar that engages the slide stop and which forms a seating for the rear end of the mainspring. A ring at the rear end fits the recess in the cam projection and receives the pin of the slide locking lever. A retaining ball is seated inside the ring, on the end of the locking lever spring, which provides the necessary ten-

sion for the operation of the slide locking lever.

9. The magazine (Fig. 7), has a capacity of 13 rounds, and consists of a tube (case), follower (platform), spring and bottom plate.

   (a) The tube (case) is of the box type, and is fluted for a short distance from its base. The bottom edges are formed into guides for the bottom plate and the mouth is shaped to retain ammunition in the magazine. A slot is cut in the right front for the engagement of the magazine catch.

   (b) The follower (platform) has a stem formed on its underside to receive the spring, and the upper surface is shaped to position ammunition in the feed way. The top front engages the slide locking lever to serve as a hold-open device.

   (c) The spring is wound of round wire, looped at each end. One end is attached around the stem of the follower (platform).

   (d) The bottom plate closes the bottom of the tube (case) and holds the spring under compression. Its edges are turned in to form guideways for the guides of the tube, and it is cut so that the center part serves as a spring clip to retain the plate in position.

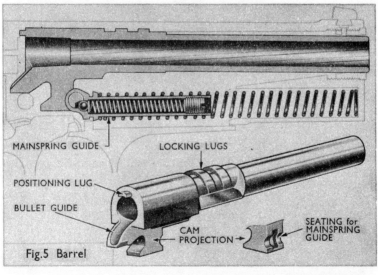

MAINSPRING GUIDE

LOCKING LUGS

POSITIONING LUG

BULLET GUIDE

CAM PROJECTION →

SEATING for MAINSPRING GUIDE

Fig.5 Barrel

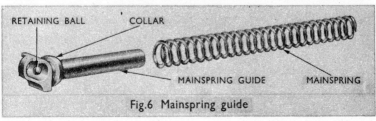

RETAINING BALL

COLLAR

MAINSPRING GUIDE

MAINSPRING

Fig.6 Mainspring guide

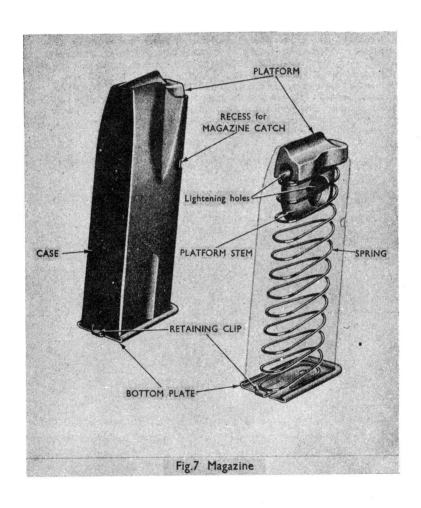

PLATFORM

RECESS for
MAGAZINE CATCH

Lightening holes

CASE

PLATFORM STEM

SPRING

RETAINING CLIP

BOTTOM PLATE

Fig.7 Magazine

Section 2, Operation:

10. To load and unload:
   (a) To load the pistol (Fig. 8), insert a filled magazine into the butt and press it fully home. The pistol is now loaded. It is safe to handle or carry in the holster, as there is no round in the chamber.
   (b) To prepare to fire (Fig. 8), point the muzzle in a safe direction, pull the slide fully to the rear, and release it sharply. This action cocks the hammer and feeds a round into the chamber. The pistol is now ready to fire. If it is not going to be fired immediately, engage the safety catch on the left side of the receiver by pushing it forward and up until it snaps into its notch on the slide.
   (c) To unload the pistol, point the muzzle in a safe direction and remove the magazine by pressing on the magazine release button on the left side of the butt. Pull back the slide to eject the live round from the chamber, and look to insure the pistol is clear of ammunition. Release the slide, insert an empty magazine and press the trigger, allowing the hammer to rotate forward under control of the thumb.

11. Precautions in handling:
   (a) When loading, preparing to fire or unloading, the finger should be kept clear of the trigger until it is necessary to place it there.
   (b) Before operating a pistol, other than firing, the magazine is removed and the pistol is examined to insure that it is clear of all ammunition.
   (c) It is a poor safety practice to carry a loaded pistol with a round in its chamber in the holster, even with the safety catch on, as the safety can work clear. It is equally poor practice to carry a loaded pistol with a round in the chamber and the hammer uncocked, as it can inadvertantly become cocked. If a pistol must be carried with a round in the chamber, put the hammer at half-cock position, and apply the safety catch.

12. Function of the pistol upon firing, (Figs. 9 and 10): With the pistol loaded, a round in the chamber and the hammer cocked, pressure on the trigger forces the tripping lever upwards, causing the sear connecting arm to rotate and operate the sear. The sear disengages from the full cock notch of the hammer, allowing the hammer to rotate sharply forward under the influence of its spring, to strike the rear end of the firing pin. Driven forward by the hammer blow, the firing pin protrudes through the firing hole and strikes the cartridge primer, thus firing the round. During this action the firing pin is compressed, and when the impulse of the hammer has been absorbed, the spring re-asserts itself, forcing the firing pin rearward into the housing.

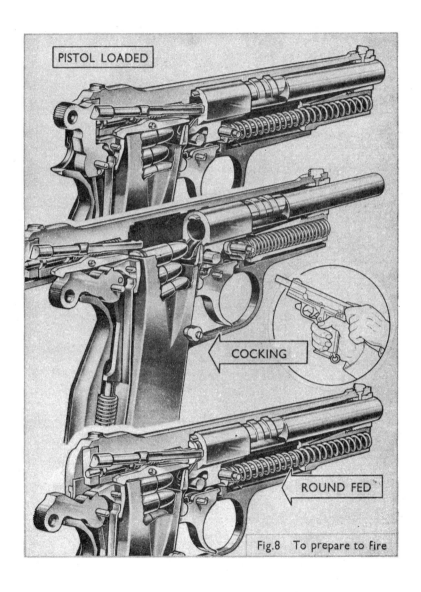

PISTOL LOADED

COCKING

ROUND FED

Fig.8 To prepare to fire

13. Function of pistol during recoil, (Figs 11 and 12): When the round is fired, the gases force the slide and barrel rearward. The barrel is locked with the slide for the initial movement of 3/16 of an inch during which travel the bullet leaves the muzzle. As the slide moves it carries with it the sear connecting arm, disconnecting the sear from the tripping lever and allowing the sear spring to re-assert itself. At the same time the rear of the slide rotates the hammer rearward.

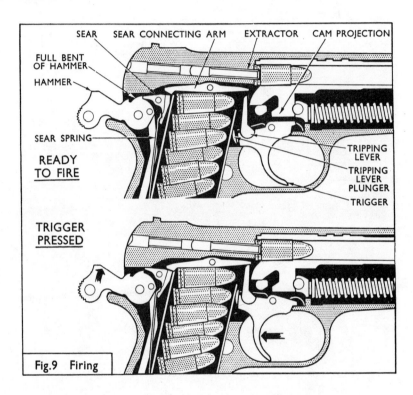

Fig.9 Firing

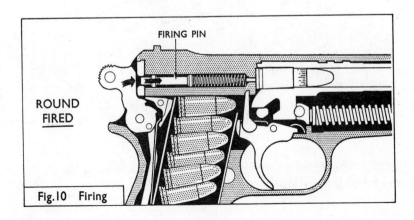

Fig.10 Firing

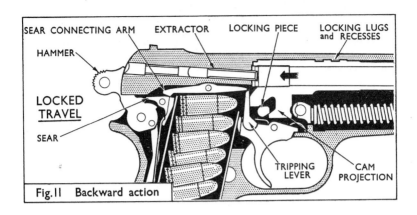

Fig.II   Backward action

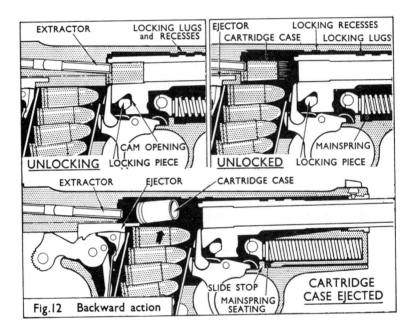

Fig.12   Backward action

(a) After the initial movement of the barrel, the cam slot engages the locking piece, causing the rear end of the barrel to move downward, disengaging the locking lugs from the locking recesses. The locking piece then contacts the end of the slot, thus preventing further movement of the barrel.

(b) Continuing its movement, the slide compresses the mainspring. The cartridge seating moves away from the chamber, carrying the cartridge case held to it by the extractor until it passes over the ejector. The case contacts the ejector and is thus ejected from the right side of the pistol slide.

(c) Continued movement of the slide causes the feed piece to move over, and clear of, the leading round in the magazine. This leaves the round free to rise under influence of the magazine spring, ready to be fed into the chamber on the forward movement. The rearward movement is arrested when the mainspring seating reaches the slide stop.

14. Function of pistol during counter-recoil, (Figs. 13 and 14):

(a) When the backward action is complete the mainspring re-asserts itself and forces the slide forward. As the slide moves, the feed piece contacts the leading round in the magazine and feeds it up into the chamber; as this happens, the cartridge case rides up the cartridge seating where it is engaged by the extractor. The rear end of the slide disengages from the hammer, allowing the hammer to rotate forward, under the influence of its spring, until its full cock notch engages the sear. The hammer is thus held in the cocked position.

(b) Continuing its movement, the slide carries the barrel with it. The locking piece engages the upper face of the cam slot, causing the rear end of the barrel to rise until the locking lugs enter their locking recesses. Barrel and slide travel locked together for 3/16 of an inch, and the top rear of the cam slot engages the top of the locking piece, retaining the barrel in the locked position. The forward movement is arrested by the pin of the slide locking lever.

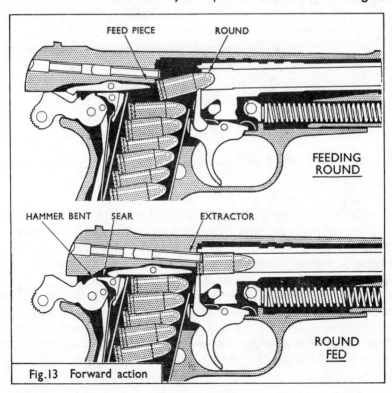

FEED PIECE   ROUND

FEEDING ROUND

HAMMER BENT   SEAR   EXTRACTOR

ROUND FED

Fig.13 Forward action

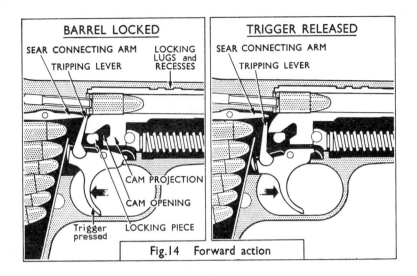

Fig.14   Forward action

15. Function of the trigger mechanism (Fig. 15):

(a) During the backward and forward motion of recoil and counter-recoil, pressure on the trigger (1) has been maintained and at the end of the forward action the sear connecting arm (2) is positioned behind the tripping lever (3). When the trigger is released, the tripping lever, under the influence of the trigger spring (4), is drawn down clear of the sear connecting arm. The plunger spring re-asserts itself, rotates the lever rearward and positions it under the forward end of the sear connecting arm, ready to commence the cycle of operations when the trigger is again pressed.

(b) The trigger must therefore be released and again pressed for each subsequent shot.

16. Function of the hold-open device, (Fig. 16):

(a) When the last cartridge case has been ejected, the magazine follower (platform) raises the lug of the slide locking lever into the recess of the slide, to hold the slide open to the rear. The movement of the locking lever rotates its pin slightly, so that the edge of the recess in the pin engages the retaining ball in the mainspring guide and slightly increases the compression of the locking lever spring.

(b) When the empty magazine is replaced by a filled one, the slide locking lever must be disengaged to allow the slide to move forward. This is done by pressing down on the thumb-piece of the lever. It can also be done by drawing back the slide slightly, so the locking lever can return to its normal position. This is effected by the influence of its spring transmitted through the retaining ball to the edge of the recess in the locking lever pin. Should the locking lever spring fail to function, the drawing back of the

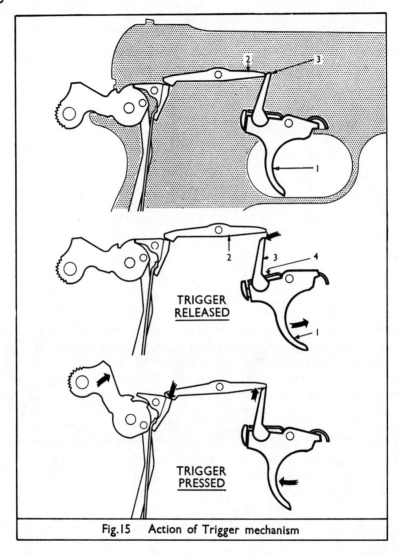

Fig. 15   Action of Trigger mechanism

slide will cause the front angle of the locking recess to bear against that on the locking lever and force the locking lever downward.

17. The safety catch (Fig. 17), cannot be applied unless the hammer is cocked and the slide is fully to the rear, or fully forward. When the safety catch is applied it enters a recess in the slide, locking the slide. Also, a stud on its inner face moves into the path of the sear to prevent its movement, thereby locking the hammer in the cocked position.

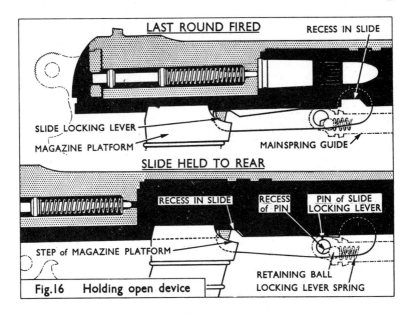

LAST ROUND FIRED — RECESS IN SLIDE

SLIDE LOCKING LEVER
MAGAZINE PLATFORM — MAINSPRING GUIDE

SLIDE HELD TO REAR

RECESS IN SLIDE — RECESS of PIN — PIN of SLIDE LOCKING LEVER

STEP of MAGAZINE PLATFORM

RETAINING BALL
LOCKING LEVER SPRING

Fig.16   Holding open device

18. The following mechanical safety features are built into the Hi-Power to insure safety to the user:

(a) The barrel and slide are locked together for the last 3/16 of an inch of the forward movement which insures that the breech is sealed before the firing pin is struck.

(b) The barrel and slide are locked together for the initial 3/16 of an inch of the rearward movement which allows time for the bullet to leave the muzzle, and for the gas pressure to drop to a safe level, before unlocking takes place.

(c) The pistol cannot be fired (Fig. 18) if the slide has not fully reached the limit of foreward movement because the sear connecting arm is not far enough forward to be operated by the tripping lever.

(d) The pistol cannot be fired (Fig. 19) if the firing pin does not receive a full blow from the hammer, because the firing pin is shorter than its housing and is held withdrawn from the firing hole by its spring.

(e) The pistol cannot be fired (Fig 20), unless the magazine is in place. This is a feature common to many European military automatic pistols, but is not usually found on U.S. Military type pistols. This feature prevents possible discharge of a round that may have been left in the chamber after the magazine has been removed. When the magazine (5) is removed, the tripping lever plunger (6) moves rearward under the influence of its spring (7) and projects into the magazine housing. This causes the tripping lever (3) to rotate forward and clear of the sear connecting arm (2)

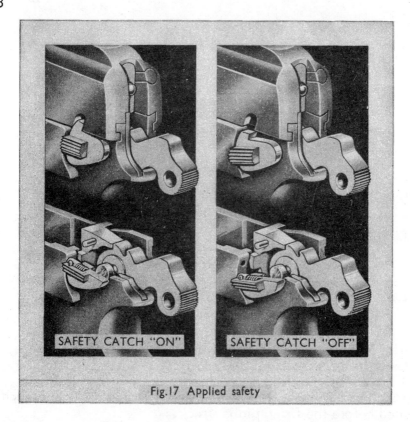

Fig.17 Applied safety

where, if the trigger (1) is pressed, the tripping lever cannot operate the sear connecting arm. When the magazine is in position its front wall forces in the tripping lever plunger, compressing its spring. The tripping lever is rotated rearward and is positioned under the forward end of the sear connecting arm.

(f) A half-cock (half-bent) (8) incorporated in the hammer (9) locks the sear (10) when engaged with it, and the hammer must be deliberately drawn back to release it from the half-cock position (Fig. 21 and 22). If the controlling thumb should slip from the comb of the hammer when in the act of cocking or lowering

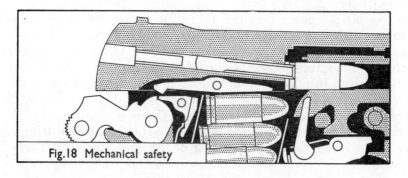

Fig.18 Mechanical safety

the hammer, the sear will engage the half-cock and in so doing prevent any danger of accidental discharge. Additionally, if a loaded pistol with the hammer forward should be dropped on the muzzle, the blow would cause the slide to move only enough to force the hammer to engage the half-cock.

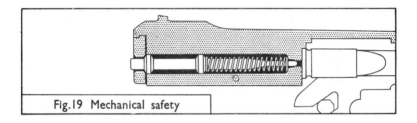

Fig.19 Mechanical safety

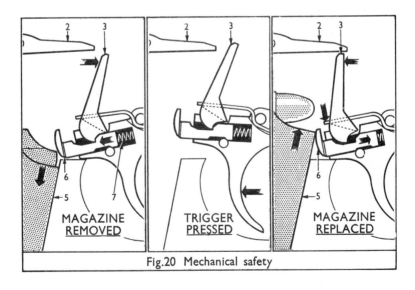

MAGAZINE
REMOVED

TRIGGER
PRESSED

MAGAZINE
REPLACED

Fig.20 Mechanical safety

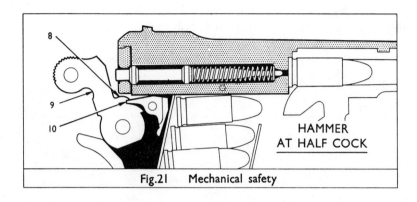

Fig.21   Mechanical safety

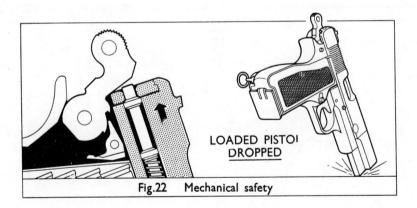

Fig.22   Mechanical safety

CHAPTER 2, STRIPPING AND SERVICING

Section I, Stripping for Cleaning in the Field:

19. Before stripping, insure that the pistol is safe to handle, by removing the magazine, pulling back the slide, and looking into the receiver to make sure the pistol is clear of ammunition.

20. To remove the magazine (Fig. 23), press in the magazine catch (11) and withdraw the magazine (5) from its housing.

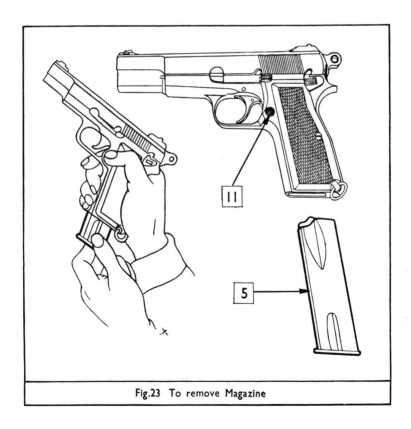

Fig.23 To remove Magazine

21. To remove the slide (12), push it fully to the rear (Fig. 24) and apply the safety catch (13) to engage its forward recess (14) in the slide. Raise the rear end of the slide locking lever (15), press inward on its pin (16) which protrudes through the right hand side of the receiver, and withdraw the slide locking lever. Hold the slide firmly, disengage the safety catch, allow the slide to move forward under control and remove it.

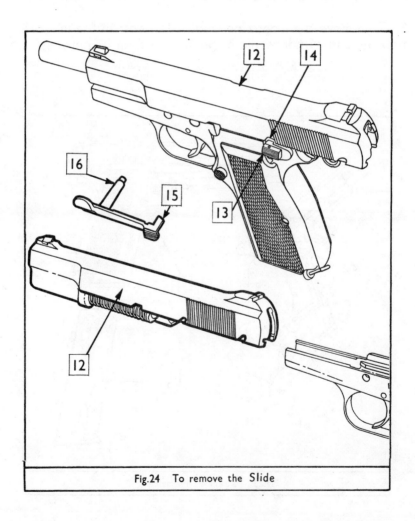

Fig.24   To remove the Slide

22. To remove the barrel (Fig. 25), hold the slide firmly (12), push the main spring guide (17) forward against the main spring (18), raise the rear end out of engagement with the cam projection (19) and withdraw the mainspring guide assembly. Disengage the rear end of the barrel (20) from its seating in the slide and withdraw the barrel.

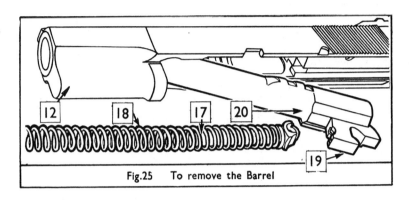

Fig.25   To remove the Barrel

23. To strip the magazine (Fig. 26), raise the retaining clip (21) of the bottom plate (22) clear of the tube (case, 23) and slide it off the tube, taking care that the spring does not fly out as the bottom plate clears it. Remove the spring and follower (25) and separate them. To avoid undue wear on the bottom plate, the magazine should not be stripped more than is necessary.

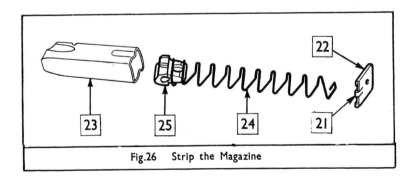

Fig.26   Strip the Magazine

24. Assembly after Field Stripping:

(a) To assemble the magazine, attach one end of the spring around the stem of the follower and insert the follower into the tube with the lightening hole in the follower facing the rear of the tube. Compress the spring and replace the bottom plate.

(b) To replace the barrel, hold the slide upside down and insert the barrel muzzle end first, so that the locking lugs engage the locking recesses. Place the front end of the mainspring into its seating, press the guide forward and engage its rear end in the cam projection. The mainspring guide can be assembled to the barrel incorrectly, so care must be taken that it is parallel to the barrel. When it is parallel it will be seen that the retaining ball is in the lower part of the ring.

(c) To replace the slide, engage the center guide of the receiver with the grooves of the slide. Push the slide rearward as far as it will go and apply the safety catch to engage in its forward recess of the slide. Insert the pin of the slide locking lever into its hole in the receiver and, with the rear of the lever raised slightly, push it fully home. It may be difficult to push the pin past the retaining ball, if so, the ball can first be depressed by the tip of the cleaning rod from the right hand side of the receiver, and the pin and rod moved past the ball together. Control the forward movement of the slide and depress the safety catch. Insert an empty magazine and press the trigger, allowing the hammer to fall under control of the thumb.

Section 2, Detail Stripping for Inspection and Repair

25. Detail stripping should be done with great care to avoid
damage to component parts, and should be done only when it
is necessary, to avoid undue wear and tear from disassembly and
assembly. Begin detail stripping by carrying out field stripping,
after first insuring the pistol is clear of all ammunition.

26. To strip the butt group (Fig. 27), unscrew the side grip screws
(26) and remove the side grips (27). Unscrew and remove the lanyard ring, if present (28).

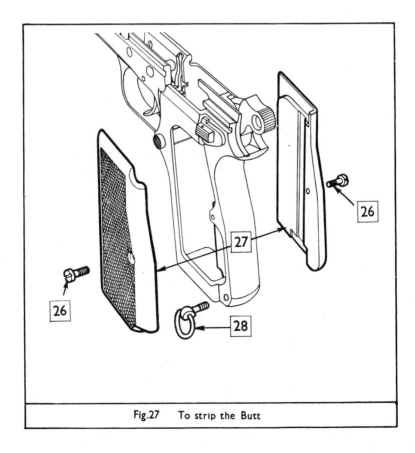

Fig.27   To strip the Butt

27. To remove the sear (Fig. 28), hold the hammer (9) to the
rear, rotate the sear (10) out of engagement with the notch of the
hammer and allow the hammer to rotate fully forward, under control.
Care must be taken to prevent the hammer from flying forward or
damage to the sear may result. Push out the sear pin (29) from the
receiver and remove the sear (10).

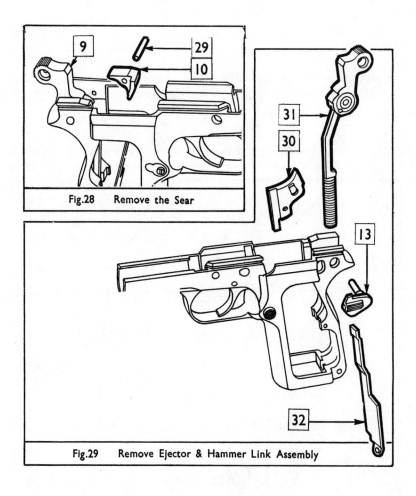

Fig.28   Remove the Sear

Fig.29   Remove Ejector & Hammer Link Assembly

28. To remove the ejector & hammer link assembly (Fig. 29),
rotate the ejector (30) fully forward. Press inward on the pin of
the safety catch (13) which protrudes through the right hand side
of the receiver and withdraw the safety catch. Remove the ejector (30), lift out the hammer link assembly (31) and the sear
spring (32).

29. To dismantle the hammer link (Fig. 30), simply screw up the retaining nut (33) until the retaining pin (34) is accessible. Remove the pin, unscrew the nut, and remove the spring (35).

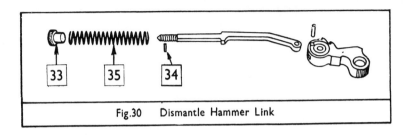

Fig.30   Dismantle Hammer Link

30. To remove and dismantle the magazine catch, push in on same (11) as far as it will go, turn the retaining catch (36) in a counter-clockwise direction until it clears the recess in the receiver and withdraw the magazine catch (11). Turn the retaining catch (36) in a clockwise direction until it clears the recess in the magazine catch and withdraw the retaining catch (36) and spring (37).

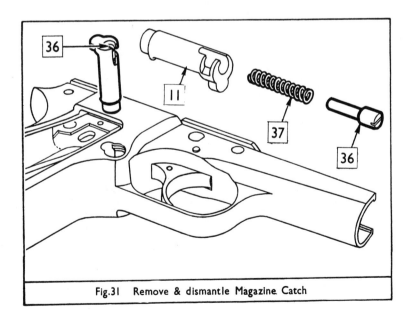

Fig.31   Remove & dismantle Magazine Catch

31. To remove the trigger assembly (Fig. 32), push out the trigger axis pin (38), rotate the tripping lever (3) rearward and lift it from the trigger (1). Pull the trigger assembly downward toward the trigger guard to remove it. It may be found necessary to press the plunger (6) against the trigger guard to give clearance for assembly.

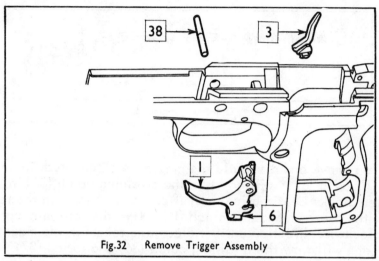

Fig.32   Remove Trigger Assembly

32. To dismantle the trigger, push out the axis pin (39) from the trigger spring (4) and remove the spring. Push out the retaining pin (40) from the tripping lever plunger (6) and withdraw the plunger (6) and spring (7). Do not strip more than is necessary.

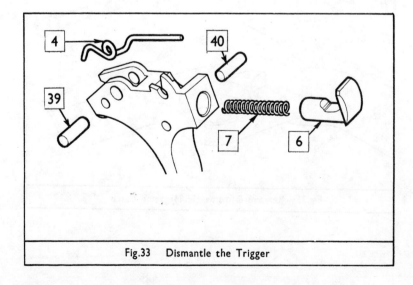

Fig.33   Dismantle the Trigger

33. To remove the firing pin (Fig. 34), press in the rear end of the firing pin (41) to clear the locking plate (42) and slide the locking plate out of the slide. Care must be taken to control the firing pin as the locking plate clears it or it will fly free and may become lost or damaged. Withdraw the firing pin (41) and spring (43).

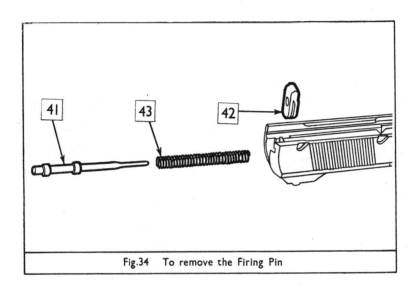

Fig.34   To remove the Firing Pin

34. To remove the extractor and sear connecting arm (Fig. 35), withdraw the extractor (44) rearward. Insert a small screw-driver in the recess in the firing pin housing and press inward on the end of the arm pin (45). Withdraw the arm pin (45) and remove the sear connecting arm (46).

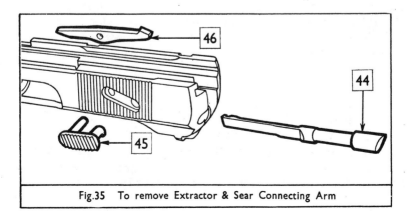

Fig.35   To remove Extractor & Sear Connecting Arm

Section 3, Inspection and Repair

35. Thoroughly clean all parts with solvent or gasoline. Check all bearing surfaces for burrs or wear. Parts which are badly damaged or worn should be replaced. Remove all rust, clean all pits.

36. All surfaces which are burred should be very carefully honed with a fine stone until original contours are reached. Examine co-related parts to ascertain if broken or worn parts are the cause of the burrs. Do not remove any more metal than is absolutely necessary.

37. Oil all parts lightly, and re-assemble as outlined in Section 4. If the pistol is to be fired, the following parts should not be oiled: bore, bullet guide, cartridge seating, magazine follower, sights and unless it is inclement weather, the exterior of the arm. If the pistol is to be stored for a great length of time, immerse the individual parts in molten grease prior to re-assembly.

Section 4, Re-Assembly of Pistol

38. To replace the sear connecting arm and extractor, lay the sear connecting arm in its seating in the slide with the sear contact to the rear. Insert the arm pin and push it fully home. Replace the extractor with the claw leading and facing inward. The extractor secures the arm pin when in position.

39. To replace the firing pin, put the firing pin spring into the housing and follow it with the firing pin. Depress the firing pin as far as possible and replace the locking plate, rounded end leading. When the plate is in position the firing pin will resume its normal position.

40. To assemble the trigger assembly, insert the tripping lever plunger and spring into the trigger. Hold the plunger firmly depressed and replace the retaining pin. Replace the trigger spring, hooked end to the front and pointing downward, and replace its axis pin.

41. To replace the trigger assembly, insert the tripping lever into its seating in the trigger and rotate it forward. Place the finger over the right hand side of the lever to prevent it from falling out and carefully replace the assembly through the trigger guard, hooking the trigger spring onto its seat in the receiver. Align the pin holes and replace the retaining pin.

42. To assemble the magazine catch, insert the retaining catch and spring into the magazine catch. Push the retaining catch inward and turn it in a counter-clockwise direction until it engages in the recess in the magazine catch.

43. To replace the magazine catch, return it to the position it originally was in the receiver. Hold the thumb piece flush to the receiver, and turn the retaining catch clockwise until it engages the recess in the receiver. Release the magazine catch.

44. To assemble the hammer link assembly, place the spring over the lower end of the link. Insert the nut in the end of the spring, compress the spring and tighten the nut until the retaining pin holes are accessible. Replace the retaining pin and unscrew the nut until its rim covers the pin.

45. To replace the hammer link and ejector, replace the sear spring with the stud on its lower end engaged in its recess in the bottom of the butt. Locate the hammer link assembly in the butt of the pistol with the spring positioned under the stop midway inside the butt. Place the ejector in the position it was removed, line up the holes, and replace the safety catch.

46. To replace the sear, rotate the ejector to its normal position. Insert the sear with the narrow part towards the hammer and the broad part placed over the sear spring. Line up the holes and replace the axis pin.

47. To assemble the butt group, replace the lanyard ring, if present. Place the side grips on the butt, leading edge first, so that the bevel on the inside surface engages under the frame of the butt. Replace the screws and tighten.

48. To complete field assembly of the major groups, see paragraph 24. If it is not desired to fire the pistol, insert an empty magazine, squeeze the trigger and allow the hammer to rotate forward under control of the thumb. Pull back the slide and depress the slide locking lever to test for functioning. Examine the pistol as a complete assembly, visually checking for proper co-relation of all parts and proper and complete assembly.

Section 5, Routine Servicing of the Pistol

49. Care must be taken in the treatment of the weapon to keep it in a condition that will give perfect functioning and continued accuracy. It is essential that the entire mechanism be kept clean and properly lubricated, so that the weapon may operate easily and to prevent stoppages.

50. Before firing, the pistol should be field stripped and all exposed parts cleaned and checked for wear and burrs. Worn or burred parts should be changed or repaired as outlined in paragraph 36, and magazines and ammunition must be cleaned and examined for damage.

51. For firing, the following parts should be lubricated with light machine oil:

        mainspring guide assembly
        interior of slide
        exterior of barrel
        guide ribs
        guide grooves
        cam projection
        locking piece
        hammer link assembly
        sear
        trigger assembly
        slide locking lever pin
        firing pin
        sear connecting arm
        magazine catch
        interior of magazine tube

52. For parts to be left dry for firing, see paragraph 37.

53. During firing, every opportunity should be taken to clean, examine and relubricate the pistol during lulls in action. Special attention should be paid to gas-effected parts. Magazines and ammunition must also be attended to.

54. After firing, field strip the pistol. Remove the barrel and scrub it with hot soapy water, dry thoroughly and oil. Clean the cartridge seating also with hot soapy water, being particularly careful to dry thoroughly before oiling. Magazines must be cleaned and oiled, and the remainder of the pistol thoroughly cleaned and re-oiled without detail stripping. The barrel must be cleaned with an oily flannel for a few days after firing.

55. When preparing the pistol for use in abnormal conditions, all working parts must be thoroughly dried before being treated with suitable lubricant. For extremely cold weather, the entire pistol is best left dry of all oil, as it can gum under the extreme cold and prevent proper functioning. Molybdenum disulphide may be used to lubricate the slide, or various commercial lubricants are available which will not gum in the cold. For extremely hot conditions, a heavier oil may be used, and for beach landings a light coating of grease may be used as protection against the salt water. For dusty and sandy climates a graphited grease is reccommended by British military sources.

56. To correct errors in elevation in the British military Hi-Power and on standard commercial models, the height of the foresight is changed. To change the sight blade in the British model, it can be drifted laterally until it is free of its slot in the front sight base. It may then be changed or altered as necessary. If a lower fore sight is installed, the mean point of impact will be raised, and vice versa. On current commercial models, the foresight is drifted free straight upward. It should not be removed unless absolutely necessary on commercial models, it is easier altered on the slide.

57. To correct errors in direction on British military Hi-powers, the front sight is drifted laterally in the front sight base, and staked in place at zero. On commercial models, the rear sight is drifted laterally in the rear sight dovetail, and staked at zero.

58. On many early and Nazi production Hi-Powers, the rear sight was a scaled-down tangent type, as is usually found on rifles and sub-machineguns. The rear sight was quickly adjustable to the desired elevation, and the front sight could be moved laterally in its slot and staked at zero. Most pistols with this tangent rear sight were also cut to accept the wooden stock, which also served as a crude holster. This has certain advantages for a military-type arm, particularly in that it extends the maximum effective range to that of a sub-machinegun. In a pistol with the large magazine capacity of the Hi-power, this is a decided advantage. Special over-size magazines have been made at FN on order and in other countries to further increase the firepower of this arm.

59. The Hi-Power pistol which has been made originally without a slot for the stock and with fixed rear sights is readily adapted to stocks as manufactured, and there are a number of commercially procurable sights which will adapt to the rear sight dovetail-type base. The stock slot is simply milled in the backstrap of the butt, and adjustable sights are mounted in the dovetail. Care must be taken to use rear sights which have a very low silhouette if the stock is also to be used as a holster. Quantities of Canadian surplus shoulder stocks for the Hi-Power have reached the surplus markets in the U.S. and abroad.

60. Because of the compact, rugged package made by the Hi-Power in the wooden stock, and because of the near-carbine potential of the arm with the stock mounted and loaded with high velocity loads, this combination has become a favorite survival and bail-out arm of bush pilots. However, it must be noted that in the U.S.A. such a combination makes a rifle with a barrel less than 16 inches in length, and as such becomes an illegal

weapon unless it is registered and a special tax paid with the Internal Revenue Service. Such a combination which is not registered is subject to seizure and forfeiture,and severe penalties can be imposed on a person possessing such an arm. In countries with more reasonable firearms regulations, however, this combination makes a highly practical survival tool.

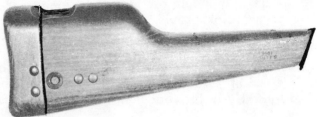

Fig. 36, Shoulder Stock Holster of Canadian Manufacture, as used on the No. I Mark I, and No. I Mark I* Hi-Power pistols.

Section 7, Special Note, Current Commercial Models:

61. Although the present manufacture of commercial Hi-Powers is essentially identical to most other production aside from very minor details such as sights, stock fittings, magazine plates and followers, trigger details and etc., an exploded view of the pistol as currently manufactured at FN is shown in Fig. 37, and a gate-fold line-drawing is shown in Fig. 38, in the rear.

62. The technical description of current production as given by the manufacturer is as follows:

Calibre	9	mm
Total length of arm . .	8	in.
Length of barrel . .	4 3/4	in.
Length of rifled part .	4	in.
Height of arm (without rearsight, with magazine)	5	in.
Width of arm (with grips)	1 1/2	in.
Width of arm (without grips)	1	in.
Number of grooves . .	6	
Direction of the grooves	right	
Twist of the grooves .	10	in.
Weight of arm (magazine empty) . . .	31	ozs
Weight of arm (magazine full)	37	ozs
Number of cartridges in magazine	13	

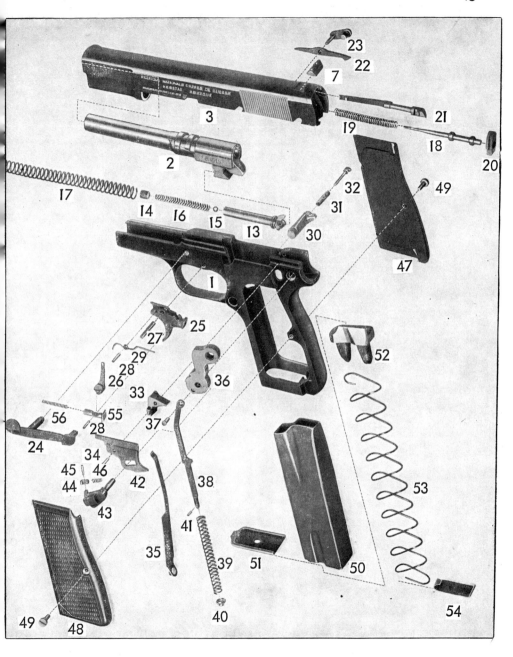

Fig. 37, Exploded View, Current Commercial Production. For Key, see paragraph 63.

63. Key to Figures 37 and 38 is as follows:

DESIGNATION	Nr of part
Frame	1
Barrel	2
Slide	3
Rearsight	7
Return spring guide	13
Return spring guide cap	14
Ball	15
Spring of return spring guide	16
Return spring	17
Firing pin	18
Firing pin spring	19
Firing pin retaining plate	20
Extractor	21
Sear lever	22
Sear lever axis pin	23
Slide stop	24
Trigger	25
Trigger lever	26
Trigger pin	27
Trigger and magazine safety pin	28
Trigger spring	29
Magazine stop	30
Magazine stop spring	31
Magazine stop spring guide	32
Sear	33
Sear pin	34
Sear spring	35
Hammer	36
Hammer pin	37
Hammer strut	38
Hammer spring	39
Hammer spring support	40
Hammer strut pin	41
Ejector	42
Safety	43
Safety stud	44
Safety pin	45
Safety spring	46
Right hand grip	47
Left hand grip	48
Grip screws (2)	49
Magazine body	50
Magazine base	51
Magazine platform	52
Magazine spring	53
Magazine bottom plate catch	54
Magazine safety	55
Magazine safety spring	56

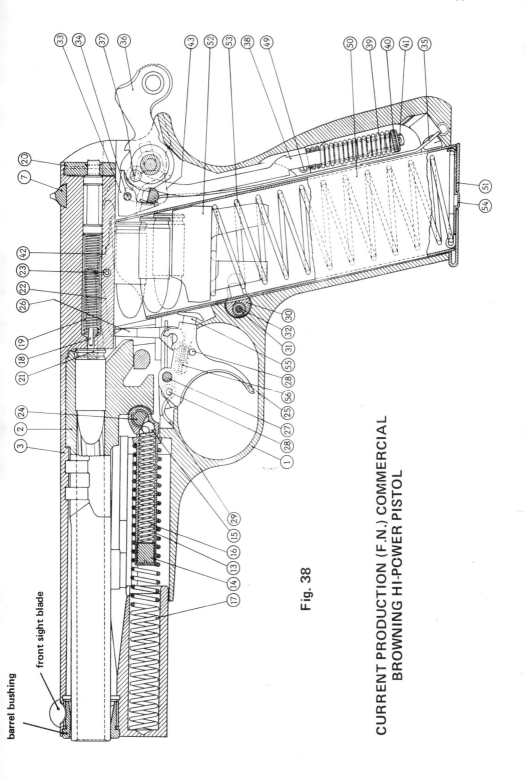

barrel bushing

front sight blade

Fig. 38

CURRENT PRODUCTION (F.N.) COMMERCIAL
BROWNING HI-POWER PISTOL